# The Coastlines of Florida

## VOLUME 1
## OF THE FLORIDA WATER STORY

**Peggy Sias Lantz and Wendy A. Hale**
**Illustrated by Jean Barnes**

Do not pick sea oats. They are protected by law.

Pineapple Press, Inc.
Sarasota, Florida

To my mother, who first taught me to love the written word. —Peggy Lantz

To Nikki and Chris, and our family's love of the sea. —Wendy Hale

To Mikey and in memory of Ruth E. and Albert G. Wilson —Jean Barnes

# TABLE OF CONTENTS

| | | | |
|---|---|---|---|
| Florida's Many Shorelines | 2 | Behind the Dunes | 18 |
| The Cooling of Florida | 3 | Estuaries | 20 |
| Barrier Islands | 4 | Salt Marshes | 22 |
| The Beach | 5 | Lagoons | 24 |
| Beach Habitats | 6 | The Mangrove Forest | 25 |
|    The Lower Beach | 6 | Protector of Land and Animals | 26 |
|    The Middle Beach | 10 | Bird Hotels | 30 |
|    The Upper Beach | 12 | The Value of Florida's Coastline | 31 |
| The Dunes | 14 | Glossary | 32 |
| Plants of the Dunes | 16 | | |

Copyright © 2014 by Peggy Sias Lantz and Wendy Hale
Illustrations © 2014 by Jean Barnes

Inquiries should be addressed to:
Pineapple Press, Inc.
P.O. Box 3889
Sarasota, Florida 34230

www.pineapplepress.com

First Edition
10 9 8 7 6 5 4 3 2 1

Design by Carol Tornatore
Illustrations colorized by Jennifer Borresen
Printed in the United States

Library of Congress Cataloging-in-Publication Data

Lantz, Peggy Sias, author.
   The coastlines of Florida / Peggy Sias Lantz and Wendy Hale. — First edition.
         pages cm. — (The Florida water story series ; volume 1)
   Summary: "The edge between land and sea provides many different habitats for special plants and animals to live. Many of them are unable to live anywhere else. Come explore the beaches, mangrove forests, estuaries, salt marshes, and lagoons of Florida's 1,100-mile-long coastline, the longest of any state except Alaska."—Provided by publisher.
      Audience: Ages 10–14.
      Audience: Grades 7 to 8.
      ISBN 978-1-56164-702-6 (pbk. : alk. paper)
1. Coastal animals—Florida—Juvenile literature. 2. Coastal ecology—Florida—Juvenile literature. 3. Natural history—Florida—Juvenile literature. 4. Coasts—Florida—Juvenile literature. I. Hale, Wendy, 1954– author. II. Title.
   QL169.L36 2014
   578.75'109759—dc23
              2014010173

# Coastlines

*f*lorida's coastline is washed by the Atlantic Ocean on the east and the Gulf of Mexico on the west. At its southern tip, between the mainland and the curving string of islands called the Florida Keys, Florida Bay connects these two large seas.

The entire coastline is wrinkled with bays and inlets, lagoons and barrier islands. It is more than 1,800 kilometers (1,100 miles) long—the longest coastline of any state except Alaska.

The edge between land and sea—where fresh waters from springs, swamps, lakes, and rivers reach the salt waters of the oceans—provides many different places, or habitats, for special plants and animals to live. Many of them are unable to live anywhere else. Come explore the beaches, the mangrove forests, and the estuaries, salt marshes, and lagoons of Florida's long coastline.

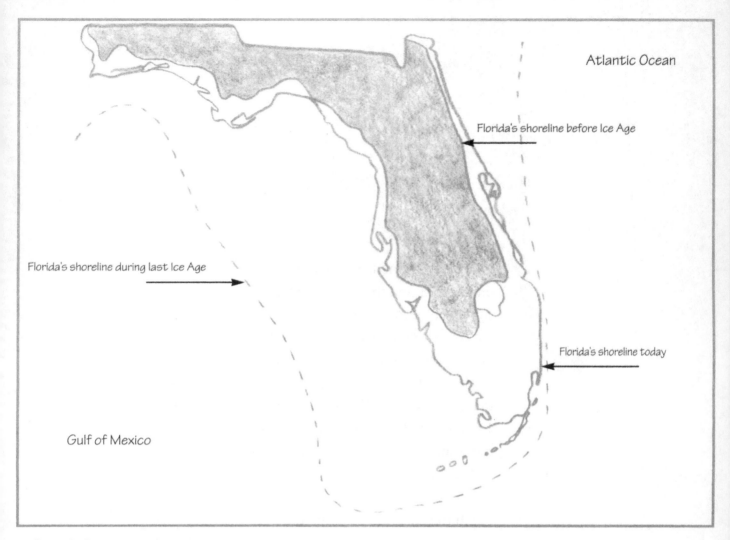

Atlantic Ocean

Florida's shoreline before Ice Age

Florida's shoreline during last Ice Age

Florida's shoreline today

Gulf of Mexico

# Florida's Many Shorelines

Millions of years ago, Florida was hardly here at all. A few small islands of the central ridge of what would one day be Florida stuck up out of the ocean. Florida's shoreline was small, because the ocean was bigger. The earth's weather was warm—warm almost to the Arctic Circle—and only a small amount of water was frozen in ice at the North and South Poles.

Then earth's weather became colder. Glaciers and icebergs formed in what is now Canada and the northern United States. The great oceans of the world shrank as their waters became bound up in ice. The water's edge receded around Florida's peninsula, and its shoreline was miles out into what is now the Gulf of Mexico and the Atlantic Ocean.

The Ice Ages came and went four times. Florida grew and shrank four times. The last Ice Age ended about ten thousand years ago. Since then, Florida's shoreline has been about like it is now. We know all this happened because scientists found a whale skeleton far inland and have found artifacts left by humans that are now under water far out in the Gulf of Mexico.

# The Cooling of Florida

The huge bodies of water that surround Florida help to keep the state mild and moist. The Atlantic Ocean and the Gulf of Mexico are so huge and deep that the water temperature stays more constant than the land. As the land heats up during the day, the hot air rises, pulling in the cooler air from over the water to replace it. At night, as the land cools below the temperature of the ocean, the breeze blows from the shore toward the water where the warmer air is rising. These pleasant breezes help keep Florida's temperatures—especially south Florida—agreeable year-round.

Clouds gather over ocean and gulf waters, blow across the land, and drop rain often. Especially in the hot summers, thunderheads billow high in the sky, sometimes causing heavy downpours and tornadoes, and making Florida the lightning capital of the United States. Hurricanes begin over the ocean during hot weather and hit Florida's coast more often than any other place in the world.

sea breeze

land breeze

# Barrier Islands

Many of the special habitats of Florida's coastline are found on barrier islands—narrow strips of land offshore that run parallel to the coast. Some barrier islands are a few miles long; some are not much bigger than sandbars. They are found along both the Atlantic coast and the Gulf coast of the state.

These islands are constantly changing. Their sands are shifted by winds, waves, tides, and storms. Sometimes during a storm, a small sandbar barrier island disappears and a new one is formed farther along the coast. Or an inlet separating two islands may be filled in or a new inlet opened up.

Barrier islands help protect the mainland of Florida from heavy waves or the storm surge that accompanies a hurricane. They are dangerous places to be when a hurricane is approaching.

Many of Florida's larger barrier islands now are connected to the mainland by bridges and are covered with houses, hotels, and condominiums. Miami Beach is a barrier island. Daytona Beach, Sanibel Island, and Marco Island are all barrier islands. Only a few of the large barrier islands are undeveloped and set aside as seaside parks and wildlife refuges.

**barrier islands**    narrow strips of land off the coast of Florida or other coastlines that run parallel to the coast.
**habitat**    a place where a plant or animal naturally grows and lives.
**inlet**    a narrow waterway opening of the coastline.

**offshore**    out in the water a distance from the shore.
**sandbar**    a ridge of sand built up by waves or currents in a b of water.
**storm surge**    the increased height of the ocean along a coa caused by a hurricane.

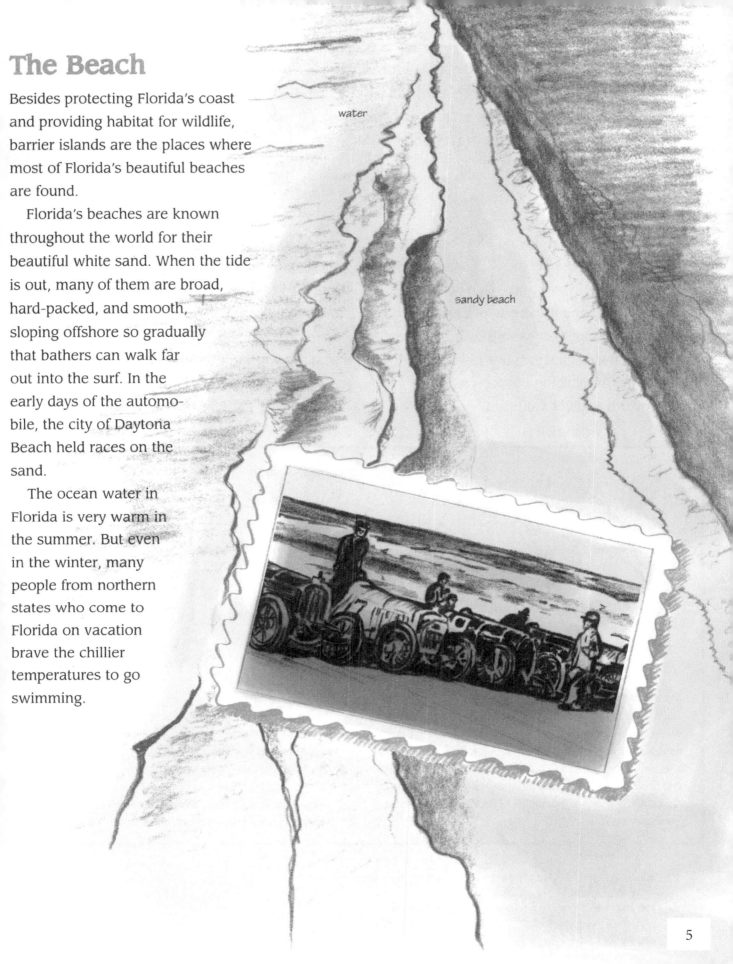

# The Beach

Besides protecting Florida's coast and providing habitat for wildlife, barrier islands are the places where most of Florida's beautiful beaches are found.

Florida's beaches are known throughout the world for their beautiful white sand. When the tide is out, many of them are broad, hard-packed, and smooth, sloping offshore so gradually that bathers can walk far out into the surf. In the early days of the automobile, the city of Daytona Beach held races on the sand.

The ocean water in Florida is very warm in the summer. But even in the winter, many people from northern states who come to Florida on vacation brave the chillier temperatures to go swimming.

water

sandy beach

# Beach Habitats

The beach contains several different habitats, including the lower beach, the middle beach, the upper beach, the dunes, and behind the dunes. The plants and animals that live in these habitats are continuously affected by the ebb and flow of both the waves and the tides.

## The Lower Beach

Waves are caused by the wind blowing across the wide sweep of the ocean. As waves approach shallow water and touch bottom, they slow down, and the crests of the waves begin to crowd together. Near the shore, the top of the water begins to move faster than the water below, causing the top water to "break" over the lower water.

The lower part of the beach is under water all the time, with waves crashing and sand churning. This tumbling lower beach is home to animals that burrow in the wet sand. Fish swim in from offshore and birds fly over the waves searching for animals to eat.

### Burrowers of the Lower Beach

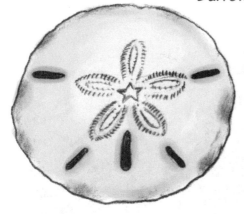

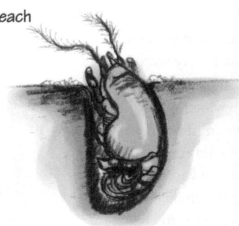

**Money at the beach**
The sand dollar is a round, flat animal. When alive, it is covered with short brown spines, but what beachcombers usually find on the beach is its skeleton, bleached white by the sun. It lives in shallow ocean waters, buried just under the sand. If you should find an unbroken sand dollar skeleton, treasure it. If you should find a live sand dollar, leave it alone.

**Crabby creature**
The mole crab burrows in the fine sand at the edge of the water. Its five pairs of legs are especially shaped for digging, and it digs into the soft sand backwards and very fast. The hard outer shell of the mole crab is about the size and shape of a pecan. Fishermen sometimes call these animals sandbugs and catch them in screened scoops to use for bait to catch fish.

---

**dune**   a ridge of sand at the ocean's edge that is piled up by the wind.

**ebb and flow**   the falling (ebb) and rising (flow) of the tides.

## Swimmers of the Lower Beach

Fish, porpoises, and sharks sometimes swim in close to the beach from the deep waters offshore to feed on smaller fish such as mullet, whiting, and pompano that swim close to shore.

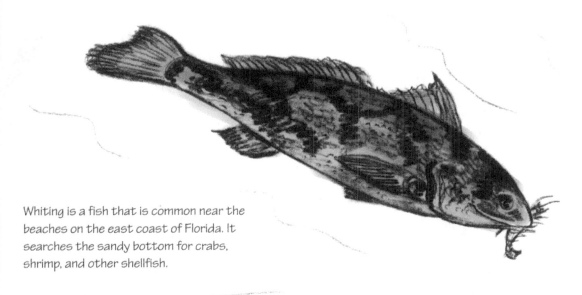

Whiting is a fish that is common near the beaches on the east coast of Florida. It searches the sandy bottom for crabs, shrimp, and other shellfish.

Florida pompano is a fish prized by surf fishermen who stand on the beach and cast their lines into the waves. The pompano's favorite food is mole crabs, and the fish will swim into water as shallow as 9 centimeters (3 inches) deep to search for them.

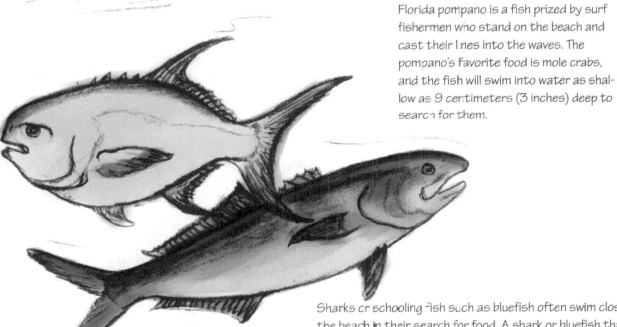

Sharks or schooling fish such as bluefish often swim close to the beach in their search for food. A shark or bluefish that bites a swimmer or surfer near the shore may mistake the person for a fish in the churning breakers.

**school**   a large number of fish of one species swimming together.

**shellfish**   an aquatic animal without a skeleton but with a shell.

## Gulls are not buoys

Gulls are properly called gulls, not seagulls, for they are found inland just as often as at sea. Several species are common along Florida's coastline all winter, including the herring gull and the ring-billed gull.

They feed on almost everything, from marine creatures and fish (both alive and dead) to picnic leftovers and garbage in landfills. They often rob other birds of their prey or follow fishing boats in large flocks, circling and squabbling for the fish scraps thrown overboard.

Gulls change their plumage many times during their lives as they mature from juvenile to adult and as summer changes to winter. Young gulls may have brown feathers instead of the gray and white of the adults. In winter a gull's black head may turn speckled or gray, and its bill may turn from red to black.

## What a funny bird!

The brown pelican is such a large and unusual bird that everyone recognizes it. It is known for its beak-with-a-pouch. Groups of pelicans are often seen flying in lines or V formation above the beach. A pelican fishes in shallow water, diving from 6 to 10 meters (20 to 30 feet) above the waves to scoop up fish in its pouch. When the pelican bobs back to the surface with a catch, water pours out of its pouch, and it juggles its meal until the fish can slide down the bird's throat head first.

Pelicans often nest in huge colonies on mangrove-forested barrier islands or on islands in lagoons, such as Pelican Island in the Indian River. Pelican Island is the nation's first wildlife refuge, set aside by President Theodore Roosevelt in 1903.

## Ha, ha, ha

The only gull that nests in Florida and lives here year-round is the laughing gull. It is named for its call, which sounds like chattering laughter. The laughing gull's handsome summertime plumage of black head and red bill and feet make the adult bird easy to identify.

Its nest is usually made of grasses and other dune plants on a sandy barrier island, with three or four eggs laid in May or June.

---

**buoy**    a floating marker tied to the bottom to mark a channel or sandbar for boats.

**marine**    in or about the sea.

**plumage**    the entire covering of feathers on a bird.

**prey**    an animal that is eaten by another animal.

**species**    a kind of plant or animal.

## A turn for a tern

Terns have coloring similar to gulls, with white, gray, and black feathers, and often red bills and legs. But terns have more pointed wings than gulls, and some have notched or forked tails, which gulls do not. They never rest on the water as gulls do.

Terns fly high over the waves with their bills pointing downward, sometimes pausing in flight to look for fish. When they spot a meal, they plunge-dive to capture it. Some terns also will feed on crabs or insects.

## The scooper skimmer

The black skimmer is a large, ternlike bird with a feature that no other bird has—the lower part of its bill is longer than the upper. It flies just above the water, skimming the waves with its lower bill hanging open, cutting the surface like a scissors. When its lower bill touches a fish or shrimp, the upper bill snaps downward to snatch the prey.

## Last and least

The least tern is properly named, for it is the smallest of terns. It is also rare, because humans compete with it for recreation and living space on Florida's beaches. It spends the winter in South America, then returns to Florida each spring to nest on sandbars, beaches, and dunes. If it cannot find a suitable natural nesting site, it may lay its eggs on a gravel rooftop!

# The Middle Beach

Tides are caused by the pull of the moon's gravity and the spinning of the earth. Two low tides and two high tides occur every day on Florida's Atlantic side. One to four tides of different heights occur on the Gulf side. Along Florida's Atlantic coast, the difference in water depth between high and low tides ranges from less than a meter (about 2 feet) near Miami to 2.5 meters (nearly 8 feet) near Jacksonville. The Gulf coast tides average less than a meter (only 2 to 3 feet) between high and low.

The middle beach is under water at high tide, but at low tide it is exposed to the hot Florida sun. Sometimes heavy rains bring fresh water into this salty environment, affecting the animals that live here.

Here, you may see birds running up and down the beach, dodging the waves. Or clams may close up their shells to keep moisture in when the tide is out, while crabs may burrow in the sand to keep from being washed away when the tide is changing.

### Hermit Crab

Some animal shells grow larger and larger as the animal grows. Others outgrow the hard shell, discard it, and build a new, bigger one. Most crabs have hard shells, but the hermit crab has a soft body. To protect itself, it hides in the empty shells of snails. When it grows too big for its borrowed house, it crawls out and finds a larger shell to live in.

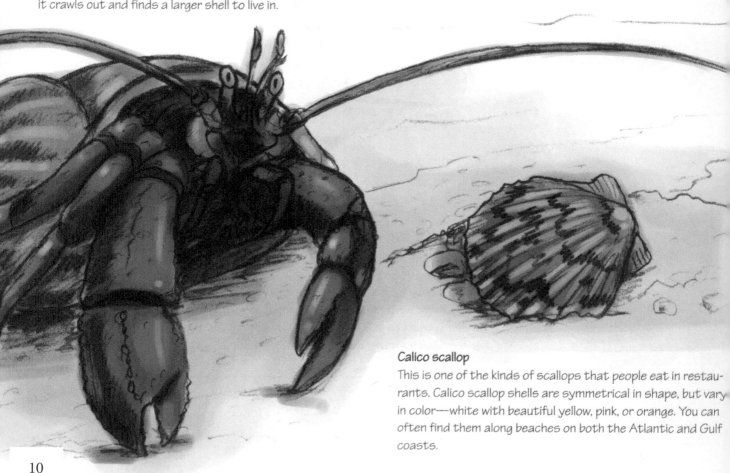

### Calico scallop

This is one of the kinds of scallops that people eat in restaurants. Calico scallop shells are symmetrical in shape, but vary in color—white with beautiful yellow, pink, or orange. You can often find them along beaches on both the Atlantic and Gulf coasts.

10

## Long-legged shorebirds

Sandpipers, willets, and lesser yellowlegs that run along the beach are all much smaller and plainer than the herons and egrets that are sometimes seen on the beach. Some shorebirds stay all year, some come for the winter, and others only pass through on migration. They wade near the edge of the surf in mixed flocks, searching for their favorite foods—marine insects, shellfish, or tiny crabs. Different shorebirds have bills and legs of different lengths, so they search for different kinds of food on different parts of the beach.

## Wave-chasers

Sanderlings are the most numerous and familiar of the small birds at the beach. Flocks of sanderlings chase up and back as the waves flow in and out, running and turning together as though performing a dance, and picking at the coquina shellfish that are uncovered as the water goes out.

sanderlings

willet

yellowlegs

sandpiper

## Coquina

The tiny coquina clam (not much bigger than your thumbnail) buries itself very rapidly as the waves recede. If you're watching closely, you can see a little squirt of water and the tiny dimple in the sand as it pulls itself down. You have to dig very fast to uncover it.

Their shells are pastel shades of pink and lavender. You can find many of them along the beach, often single shells, but sometimes two shells still attached in a pair and opened up like a butterfly. Coquina shells were used hundreds of years ago by the European settlers in Florida to make a rock-hard building material for houses and for the fort at St. Augustine.

## Lettered olive

Smooth, glossy olive shells can be found washed up on Florida beaches. Lettered olives burrow deep in the sand and live together in colonies. They feed on dead crabs and clams.

**migration**   moving from one place to another with the seasons.

# The Upper Beach

The upper beach is the area where the highest tides have reached, leaving a line of debris called sea wrack that drifts in from the ocean. Insects live in the decaying seaweed, and other animals forage for the insects. The sand is softer here, only occasionally packed hard by the waves.

### Spooks!

Ghost crabs can be seen on the beach late in the evening. The ghost crab is ghostly white or sandy-colored and almost invisible as it scurries sideways across the sand. The ghost crab has gills that must stay wet in order for it to breathe, so it feeds on marine creatures in the cool of the night when the sun won't dry it out. It can live in the water or in the moist sand. When it outgrows its old shell, it crawls out and its body expands before its new, bigger shell hardens.

**debris**   an accumulation of plant, animal, or rock fragments.

**sea wrack**   debris from the ocean piled up in a row by wind and water.

## Sargassum weed

The sargassum seaweed that grows and floats in huge mats in the Atlantic Ocean often breaks loose in rough seas and washes ashore. After a storm, you can find it along the beach in a long, brownish green drift line. If you turn over the seaweed and search among its leathery leaves, you will see the little brown balls filled with air that keep sargassum afloat. You might find other things, too—insects, crabs, or maybe a sea horse.

## Sandfleas

Sometimes called sandhoppers, these little crustaceans burrow in the sand above the high tide mark, hopping about mostly at night and feeding on dead animal matter washed up by the waves. They are not insects and do not suck blood like the fleas on a dog, though they look something like a flea and can jump like one. They are also larger than a dog flea — 2 to 3 centimeters (up to an inch).

## Oceangoing beans

Sometimes sea beans fall off vines and trees growing near the ocean in South America, Africa, and Australia and travel the world on the ocean waves. They can drift for many months and float as far as Florida. You may find some in the sea wrack washed up on the beach.

**crustacean**   a usually aquatic animal with an outside skeleton, such as lobsters and shrimp.

**drift line**   debris piled up in a row by wind and water; sea wrack.

13

# The Dunes

Beyond the reach of the waves except during storms, the dunes rise in high mounds of soft, deep sand. Blown and piled up by the wind, dunes protect the plants and animals that live behind them from the salt spray, and provide a hot, desertlike habitat for an entirely different group of plants and animals.

### Home from the sea

Loggerhead sea turtles lay their eggs on Florida's east coast beaches. Scientists know little about the turtles' lives in the deep ocean but are able to study them when the females come ashore in the summertime to lay their eggs. We do know that female sea turtles travel the seas for many miles and many years before they find their way back to the same beach where they were born to bury their eggs.

The adult loggerhead sea turtle can weigh over 150 kilograms (300 pounds), and its shell grows to over a meter (4 feet) long. Its large, blunt head gives it its name. The female comes ashore at night anytime from April to August, usually on a high tide. She leaves a broad track in the sand as she crawls to the upper beach near the edge of the dune. Her instinct tells her that she must make her nest above the high tide level so that her eggs are not washed away. Here, she digs a hole with her hind flippers and deposits up to 100 golf ball-sized eggs in it. Then she covers the hole and crawls back to the sea. Her heavy body and swimming flippers make her efforts on land difficult and slow. She may come ashore several times during the summer to lay more than one nest of eggs.

The sand, heated by the sun, keeps the eggs warm. Two to three months later, the baby turtles, small enough to fit in a tablespoon, hatch all together one night and dig their way up through the sand. They are attracted to the shine of moon and stars on the water and scramble for the safety of the waves. But if they are attracted by streetlights or hotel signs instead and do not find their way to the water, they may be eaten by raccoons or ghost crabs at night, or die from the hot sun or be eaten by gulls the next day.

Atlantic green turtles, hawksbills, and leatherbacks nest on Florida beaches, too, but only rarely and in much smaller numbers than the loggerhead.

### Turtle watch

Seeing one of these huge reptiles lumber up the beach, dig its nest hole, and lay its eggs is fascinating. Guides take groups of people on Florida beaches during turtle-nesting season and talk about sea turtles as they walk along the beach looking for a track. Only the guide carries a flashlight, for the turtles will turn back to the sea if disturbed by lights or activity on their way up the beach. If a female has already dug her nest hole and begun to lay her eggs, however, she will finish laying and cover the hole even while people are watching.

15

# Plants of the Dunes

Plants that grow on the dunes of Florida must be able to survive salt spray, hot sun, and shifting sand. Occasionally plants will be washed over with salt water from storm waves.

Do not pick sea oats. They are protected by law.

### Not for breakfast

One of these dune plants is sea oats, far different from the oatmeal or Cheerios you eat for breakfast. It has far-reaching roots that hold it in place in the loose sand, and its blossoms and seed heads bend with the wind on tall, thin stems. It helps protect the sand dunes from washing and blowing away.

### Morning brightener

Beach morning glory is sometimes called railroad vine because it clambers and stretches over the sand dunes in long lines like a railroad track. The vine grows roots where each leaf attaches to anchor the vine to the sand. Lavender, funnel-shaped flowers open in the early morning and close by noon.

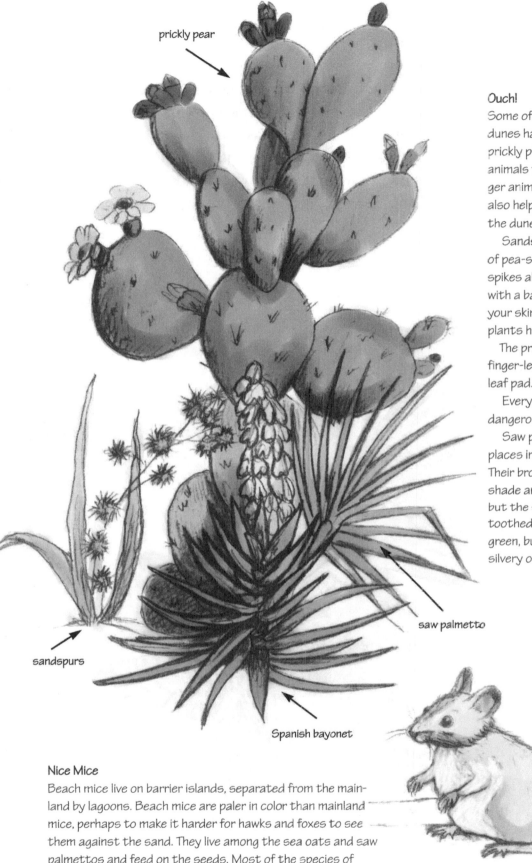

prickly pear

sandspurs

saw palmetto

Spanish bayonet

## Ouch!

Some of the plants that live on the dunes have sharp points on them. These prickly plants help protect small beach animals that hide among them from bigger animals that might eat them. They also help to keep people from walking over the dunes and disturbing the plants.

Sandspurs are grasses with clusters of pea-sized seeds that have short spikes all around them. If you step on one with a bare foot, it can stick painfully in your skin. The roots of these grassy plants help to hold the sand in place.

The prickly pear cactus has several finger-length thorns on each fleshy leaf pad.

Every leaf of the Spanish bayonet is a dangerous spear as long as your leg.

Saw palmettos grow thickly in many places in Florida, including beach dunes. Their broad leaves, called fronds, offer shade and shelter to small animals, but the stems of the fronds are saw-toothed. Most saw palmettos are shiny green, but in some areas the fronds are silvery or bluish.

## Nice Mice

Beach mice live on barrier islands, separated from the mainland by lagoons. Beach mice are paler in color than mainland mice, perhaps to make it harder for hawks and foxes to see them against the sand. They live among the sea oats and saw palmettos and feed on the seeds. Most of the species of Florida beach mice are endangered.

17

# Behind the Dunes

The habitat behind the dunes may be another dune, a strand of ocean scrub plants, a cabbage palm forest, a salt marsh of grasses and reeds, or a lagoon.

The plants that grow behind the dunes or on a second dune ridge are scrubby and stunted by salt spray. Their habitat is not quite as harsh as the beach and front dunes, but life here is not easy either. Small, straggly oak trees lean away from the constant sea-wind. Dwarf saw palmettos grow close together. Sometimes forests of cabbage palm trees with vines and beauty berry bushes cover the back of the dune.

cabbage palm

sea oats

dunes

Spanish bayonet

**lagoon**  a shallow water body partly surrounded by land that shelters it from the sea.

**strand**  a long, thin strip of land bordering a body of water.

**reed**  a tall, grasslike plant that grows in wet places.

# Estuaries, Salt Marshes, and Lagoons

A barrier island may be separated from the mainland by an estuary, a salt marsh, or a lagoon. A long stretch of salt marshes also extends along the "bend" of Florida's Gulf coast, where there are no barrier islands. All of these habitats are places where salt water from the sea and fresh water from rivers and streams come together. The water in a lagoon or estuary is less salty than the sea and more salty than the fresh water running off the land.

Detritus washed off the land and plankton from the sea mix together in these watery places to form a soup that is rich in nutrients. This soup feeds microscopic animals, insects, and fish, which, in turn, are food for larger fish, birds, and mammals. Estuaries, salt marshes, and lagoons are very important in this cycle of life called the food chain.

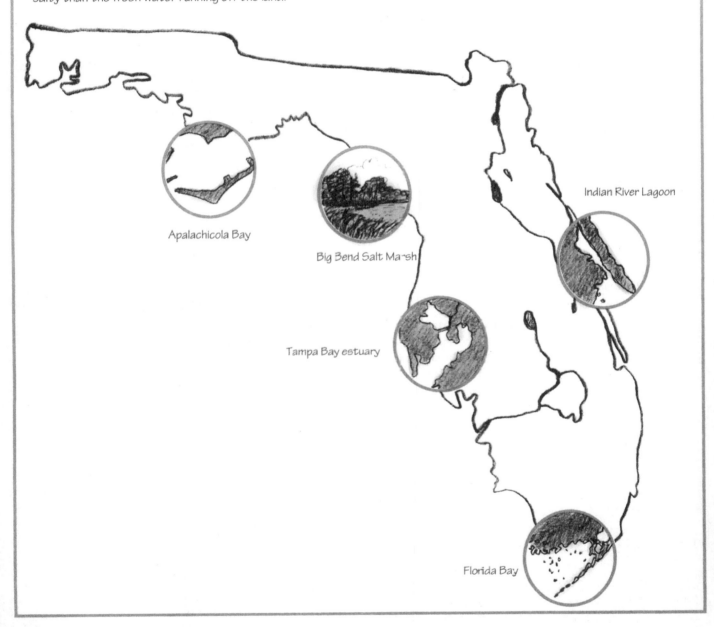

Apalachicola Bay

Big Bend Salt Marsh

Tampa Bay estuary

Indian River Lagoon

Florida Bay

**detritus**   particles of decayed animals and plants.
**estuary**   the watery area where a river meets the sea, where river flow meets the tide, and where fresh water meets salt water
**food chain**   the passage of food energy from plants, which make their own food from the energy of the sun, to animals that eat plants, to animals that eat other animals.

**microscopic**   too small to be seen without a magnifying lens.
**nutrients**   foods that promote growth.
**plankton**   microscopic plants and animals that drift in the sea.

# Estuaries

Estuaries are places where a river meets the sea. The river current flowing outward meets the incoming tide to make a constantly changing mixture of saltiness. Some scientists think that estuaries are the most productive places in the world, where the young of many species hatch and grow, and where many species of crabs, oysters, and clams live out their lives.

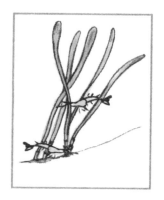

## Underwater grassy meadows

Though the long, thin blades of sea grasses make them look like an overgrown lawn, they are not real grasses at all. They are a kind of plant—in fact, the only plant—that flowers and produces fruits and seeds in seawater. Florida's shallow estuaries have some of the biggest seagrass beds in the world. Most of the sea grasses grow in Florida Bay and near the coral reefs. The several species of sea grasses that occur in Florida provide food and shelter to most species of fish and shellfish during some part of their lives.

## The journey of the pink shrimp

The female pink shrimp lays her eggs in deep ocean waters near south Florida. When the larvae hatch, they begin swimming and floating with the currents. They feed at night on plankton, shedding their shells as they outgrow them. About a month later, the young shrimp enter one of the shallow, grassy estuaries along the southwest coast of Florida. Here they feed on organisims on the seagrass blades and in the mud, growing to about 5 centimeters (2 inches) long in about two months. Then most of them leave the estuary, migrating back to the ocean on the falling tides. Those that are not eaten by snook and other fish, or are not netted by shrimp fishermen, may reach deep water again, growing bigger all the time. If they escape the commercial shrimp trawlers offshore, they continue to grow to as long as 18 centimeters (6 inches). In the spring, the females lay their eggs again in the waters off south Florida.

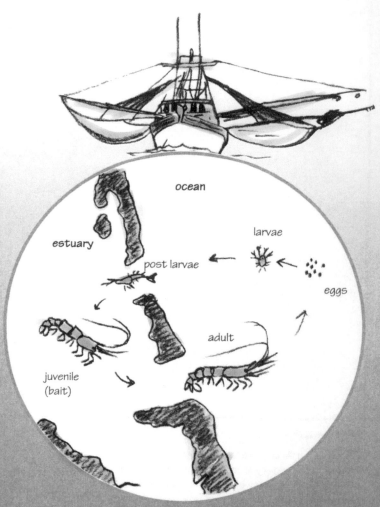

ocean

estuary

larvae

post larvae

eggs

adult

juvenile (bait)

20    **larvae**    *the immature forms of an animal that are very different from the adult forms.*

### Blue crab

The blue crab lays its eggs in the sea far from the barrier islands. When the crab larvae hatch from the eggs, they float into the marshes and estuaries with the tides and feed on detritus in the muddy and sandy bottoms. A new generation of crabs then returns to the sea to lay eggs. Fishermen capture blue crabs in special baited boxes for people to eat.

### Horseshoe crab

Horseshoe crabs live their lives in the ocean, then return to the estuaries and marshes on moonlit nights to mate and lay their eggs in the sand. These strange animals, with long, spiked tails and horseshoe-shaped shells, have ancient ancestors. Similar-looking fossils date back hundreds of millions of years. Horseshoe crabs are not true crabs. Their closest relatives are spiders and scorpions!

### Oysters

Oysters are special seafood treats for many people. They are bivalves, with two matching shells that can be closed tightly for safety. They eat by sucking in seawater and filtering out nutrients. Many of Florida's oysters live their lives in a huge estuary at the mouth of the Apalachicola River in the Panhandle.

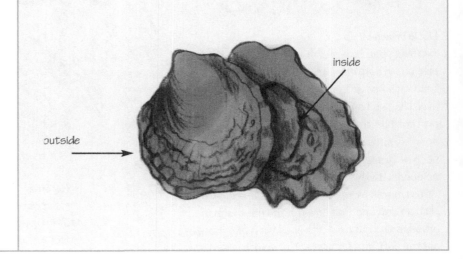

inside

outside

**bivalve**   an animal with two matching shells hinged together, such as a clam.
**filtering**   separating out particles from water.

**fossil**   a mineralized piece of a plant or animal from a past age. *Mineralized* means that, over a long time, hard nonliving material replaces soft living material.

21

# Salt Marshes

Along some parts of Florida's flat coastline, the ocean tides flow inland over a large area, leaving the soil salty. The tides are shallow and the waves are small, leaving calm waters where certain sea grasses and animals can survive. These are the salt marshes.

Grasses called needlerush and cordgrass grow in some marshes. Leatherfern or sawgrass grow in others. A lone cabbage palm sometimes stands in the marsh.

Saltwater organisms that ride in on the tides find food and hiding places here. Insects, spiders, snails, crabs, and birds such as sparrows and wrens graze on the grasses or eat the algae and microscopic organisms in the marsh.

wren

sparrow

clapper rail

### Little brown birds

Seaside sparrows and marsh wrens live nowhere else but in salt marshes. The sparrow's nest is lined with fine grass, and it often has a canopy over the top to hide it from predators and to protect the chicks from the sun. The seaside sparrow eats many different small creatures such as grasshoppers, snails, and spiders, as well as seeds. It has a buzzy call.

The marsh wren builds a coconut-shaped nest with an entrance in the side. The nest is made of grasses and cattails and lined with fine grasses, cattail fluff, and feathers. The marsh wren eats aquatic insects such as dragonflies and mosquito larvae, and its song is a bubbly trill.

### Noisy bird

The clapper rail is a brownish, chickenlike bird that builds its nest in grasses or reeds in the salt marsh. It weaves the stalks into an overhead canopy so the nest cannot be easily seen from above. Eggs are laid in the spring, and the chicks leave the nest immediately after hatching. Although the rail is rarely seen, its clacking call can be heard in the marsh every few minutes most of the year. It feeds on crabs, snails, grasshoppers, and worms.

*organism*   a living plant or animal.

Creeks and rivers often run through the marshes, providing deeper water where fish and other ocean animals come in to lay eggs, hunt for food, or hide. Many offshore animals begin their lives in the salt marsh. Manatees live here. Land animals such as raccoons and skunks often come into the salt marsh to find food.

### The Mosquito

The saltmarsh mosquito is one of the most annoying of all the 69 species of mosquitoes in Florida. It hatches in salt marshes and is blown by the wind or flies to inland places where the female bites people and animals. But the mosquito also is food for hundreds of species of fish and birds, in both its larval and adult stages.

### The turtle

The diamondback terrapin is a turtle that lives in the salt waters of estuaries, salt marshes, and lagoons. It has special glands near its eyes to get rid of the salt, and a diamond-shaped pattern of growth rings on its shell.

### The snake

The saltmarsh snake is related to Florida's other water snakes, but is the only Florida species that can live in salt water. It is not poisonous. It eats minnows and other small animals and is rarely seen during the day.

**growth rings**   layers that are produced in a single growing period in a tree or animal shell.

# Lagoons

A shallow body of water between a large barrier island and the mainland may be called a lagoon, a bay, or a sound. It may be nearly enclosed by sandbars. Or it may run for miles—as does the Indian River lagoon—as a long inland waterway.

Lagoons provide protection for young aquatic animals because the water is often too shallow for larger fish that might eat them. The water inside a lagoon is calmer, too, buffered from the heavy wave action of the sea by a barrier island or sandbars.

The Indian River lagoon on the east coast of Florida runs for 260 kilometers (160 miles) from New Smyrna Beach to Jupiter Inlet.

Sea turtles, manatees, mullet, shrimp, horseshoe crabs, and many other animals rely on the special waters of lagoons for all or a part of their lives.

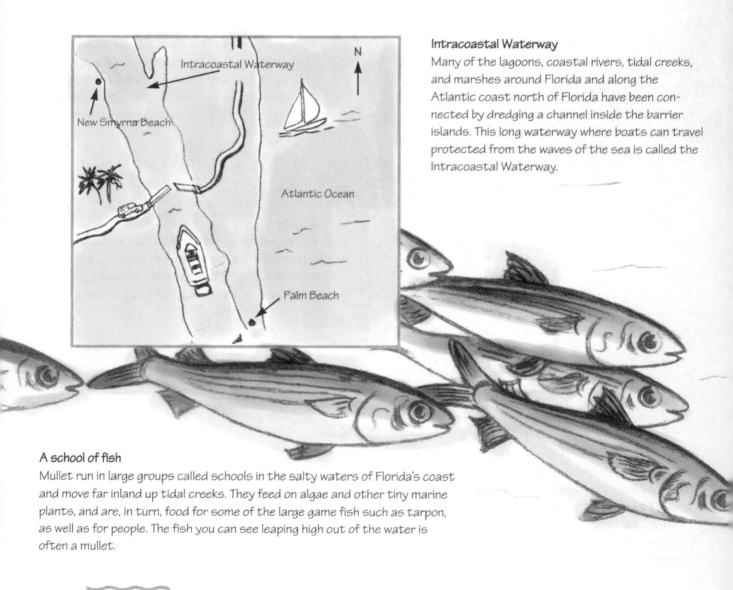

### Intracoastal Waterway
Many of the lagoons, coastal rivers, tidal creeks, and marshes around Florida and along the Atlantic coast north of Florida have been connected by dredging a channel inside the barrier islands. This long waterway where boats can travel protected from the waves of the sea is called the Intracoastal Waterway.

### A school of fish
Mullet run in large groups called schools in the salty waters of Florida's coast and move far inland up tidal creeks. They feed on algae and other tiny marine plants, and are, in turn, food for some of the large game fish such as tarpon, as well as for people. The fish you can see leaping high out of the water is often a mullet.

**sound** or **bay**   a shallow body of water between a large barrier island and the mainland.

# The Mangrove Forest

Mangrove forests in Florida are found mainly on the state's southern coasts, for mangroves are trees that need warm weather and warm water.

Mangroves can live in salt water. They can live in fresh water, too, but they have more space if they grow in the salty, tide-washed areas of the coast because few other trees can grow there. Mangroves manage the salt in two different ways. The red mangrove filters out salt from the water at the surface of its roots. Black and white mangroves get rid of salt from the undersides of their leaves. Three species of mangroves grow in Florida.

### Red

The red mangrove usually grows closest to the water's edge, where the tides wash in and out twice each day. When the tide comes in, thousands of red mangrove islands in Florida Bay are flooded, with no dry land anywhere under them. Birds can nest here in greater safety, because it is harder for predators to reach the forest through the high water. The red mangrove tree is easily recognized by its strange, stiltlike prop roots, which make it look as though it is walking on the water.

red mangrove

black mangrove

### Black

The black mangrove usually is found growing inland of the red mangrove, on more sheltered, slightly higher ground. It can be recognized by the pencil-like air roots that stick up out of the mud below the trees. It withstands the chill of winter as far north as Cape Canaveral on the east coast and Cedar Key on the west coast.

### White

The white mangrove grows even farther inland on higher ground where the action of waves and tides is small. It has no unusual root features, but it has two "bumps" near the base of each leaf that help it get rid of salt.

white mangrove

**prop root**   the curving support of a red mangrove tree.   25

# Protector of Land and Animals

Mangrove forests are very important to the coastline of Florida. They help to hold shorelines in place during storms, preventing sand from washing away. They slow down floodwaters and reduce the destruction of heavy waves. They filter pollutants out of the water. They trap mud, leaves, and other debris among their prop roots and trunks. The leaves, flowers, insects, and other litter that fall from mangroves are an important part of the food chain, eaten by tiny, microscopic organisms, young fish and shrimp, and many other animals. The trees provide hiding places for small and young animals.

The mangrove forest is a nursery for young shrimp, spiny lobsters, snook, and snapper that feed and hide among the tree roots. Lizards, frogs, striped skunks, river otters, and the Everglades mink find a home in the mangrove forest. Fish swim among the prop roots of red mangroves, and oysters and sponges settle in the water beneath the trees.

**The croc**

The American crocodile is related to the alligator, but has a more pointed snout and greener color. It is endangered. Perhaps 1,000 live in the salt waters of the Florida Keys and the Everglades. American crocodiles feed mainly on fish and often swim in the mangrove creeks. The female crocodile builds a nest in the mud that is 1.5 meters (5 feet) to more than 7 meters (20 feet) across and half a meter (2 feet) or more high. She lays 20 to 80 eggs in the mound.

**nursery**   an area where the young of an animal lives during the early part of its life.

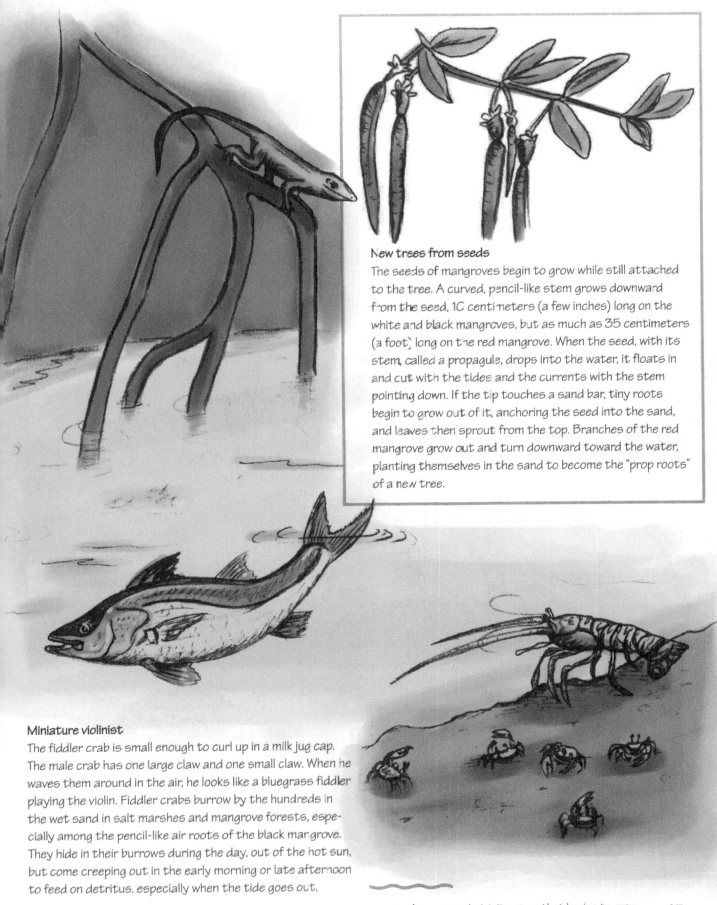

### New trees from seeds

The seeds of mangroves begin to grow while still attached to the tree. A curved, pencil-like stem grows downward from the seed, 10 centimeters (a few inches) long on the white and black mangroves, but as much as 35 centimeters (a foot) long on the red mangrove. When the seed, with its stem, called a propagule, drops into the water, it floats in and out with the tides and the currents with the stem pointing down. If the tip touches a sand bar, tiny roots begin to grow out of it, anchoring the seed into the sand, and leaves then sprout from the top. Branches of the red mangrove grow out and turn downward toward the water, planting themselves in the sand to become the "prop roots" of a new tree.

### Miniature violinist

The fiddler crab is small enough to curl up in a milk jug cap. The male crab has one large claw and one small claw. When he waves them around in the air, he looks like a bluegrass fiddler playing the violin. Fiddler crabs burrow by the hundreds in the wet sand in salt marshes and mangrove forests, especially among the pencil-like air roots of the black mangrove. They hide in their burrows during the day, out of the hot sun, but come creeping out in the early morning or late afternoon to feed on detritus, especially when the tide goes out.

**propagule**   a seed with its stem that begins to grow while still attached to the tree.

### Dear little deer

The Key deer lives only in the Florida Keys, searching the mangrove swamps for food and hiding places. It is the size of a large dog—a miniature of the white-tailed deer that lives all over the eastern United States. It may be the only mammal that can safely drink salt water, for sources of fresh water on the Keys are few. The slender legs of the Key deer can scramble over the tangle of red mangrove prop roots amazingly fast. It is an endangered species, and has a national refuge to protect it.

### Turtles and snakes

The mangrove diamondback terrapin and the mangrove saltmarsh snake live only in the mangrove forests of Florida Bay. They are only a little different from their saltmarsh cousins. This terrapin is different from other diamondback terrapins because it has raised bumps down the ridge of its shell.

The mangrove snake is usually dark with splotches on its back and light stripes along its neck. It is the only water snake that occurs in the mangroves.

## Rosie

One of the most beautiful of Florida's mangrove-nesting birds is the roseate spoonbill. Its feathers are pink and bright red. Its broad, flattened, spoon-shaped bill is grayish brown, and it hunts for food by swishing its bill from side to side through the mud or shallow water. It builds its deep nest of sticks in the mangroves in Florida Bay and along the coast of south Florida, and may share its tree with the nests of ibis or herons.

## Vireo

The black-whiskered vireo also nests in Florida's mangrove forests. It raises its family in the summertime and migrates to South America in the winter.

## Cuckoo!

The mangrove cuckoo, as you can tell by its name, lives among the mangroves of Florida Bay and the Keys. It eats caterpillars and usually stays well hidden among the leaves.

# Bird Hotels

Thousands of long-legged wading birds roost for the night and nest in colonies in mangrove forests. Sometimes the birds settle in such great flocks that the branches break. In the early 1900s, millions of birds nested in mangrove rookeries in south Florida, but human activities have reduced their numbers.

Most of these wading birds raise their young in the winter and spring dry season—December through May—when it is easier for them to catch the fish that crowd together in the shrinking ponds. They often fly far inland searching for food for their nestlings.

**colonies**   groups of the same kinds of animals living together.

**rookeries**   colonies of nesting birds.

# The Value of Florida's Coastline

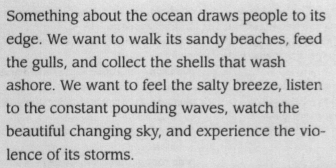

Something about the ocean draws people to its edge. We want to walk its sandy beaches, feed the gulls, and collect the shells that wash ashore. We want to feel the salty breeze, listen to the constant pounding waves, watch the beautiful changing sky, and experience the violence of its storms.

We want to live near the water. In fact, too many of us want to live near it, and much of Florida's coastline no longer provides a home to plants and animals that can live nowhere else—because we have cut down mangroves to see the water and filled in the salt marshes so we can build a house or get rid of the mosquitoes that hatch there.

We hope this book will help you care about the special places along Florida's long coastline and the plants and animals that live there.

# Glossary

**barrier islands**   narrow strips of land off the coast of Florida or other coastlines that run parallel to the coast.

**bay**   a shallow body of water between a large barrier island and the mainland.

**bivalve**   an animal with two matching shells hinged together, such as a clam.

**buoy**   a floating marker tied to the bottom to mark a channel or sandbar for boats.

**colonies**   groups of the same kinds of animals living together.

**crustacean**   an aquatic animal with an outside skeleton, such as lobsters and shrimp.

**debris**   an accumulation of plant, animal, or rock fragments.

**detritus** (de-TRY-tus)   particles of decayed animals and plants.

**drift line**   debris piled up in a row by wind and water; sea wrack.

**dune**   a ridge of sand at the ocean's edge that is piled up by the wind.

**ebb and flow**   the falling (ebb) and rising (flow) of the tides.

**estuary**   the watery area where a river meets the sea, where river flow meets the tide, and where fresh water meets salt water.

**filtering**   separating out particles from water.

**food chain**   the passage of food energy from plants, which make their own food from the energy of the sun, to animals that eat plants, to animals that eat other animals.

**fossil**   a mineralized piece of a plant or animal from a past age. *Mineralized means that, over a long time, hard nonliving material replaces soft living material.*

**growth rings**   layers that are produced in a single growing period in a tree or animal shell.

**habitat**   a place where a plant or animal naturally grows and lives.

**inlet**   a narrow waterway opening of the coastline.

**lagoon**   a shallow water body partly surrounded by land that shelters it from the sea.

**larvae** (LARV-eye)   the immature forms of an animal that are very different from the adult forms.

**marine**   in or about the sea.

**microscopic**   too small to be seen without a magnifying lens.

**migration**   moving from one place to another with the seasons.

**nursery**   an area where the young of an animal lives for the early part of its life.

**nutrients** (NOO-tree-ints)   foods that promote growth.

**offshore**   out in the water a distance from the shore.

**organism**   a living plant or animal.

**plankton**   microscopic plants and animals that drift in the sea.

**plumage**   the entire covering of feathers on a bird.

**prey**   an animal that is eaten by another animal.

**prop root**   the curving support of a red mangrove tree.

**propagule**   a seed with its stem that begins to grow while still attached to the tree.

**reed**   a tall, grasslike plant that grows in wet places.

**rookeries**   colonies of nesting birds.

**sandbar**   a ridge of sand built up by currents in a body of water.

**school**   large number of fish of one species swimming together.

**sea wrack**   debris from the ocean piled up in a row by wind and water.

**shellfish**   an aquatic animal without a skeleton but with a shell.

**sound**   a shallow body of water between a large barrier island and the mainland.

**species** (SPEE-sheez)   a kind of plant or animal.

**storm surge**   the increased height of the ocean along a coast caused by a hurricane.

**strand**   a long, thin strip of land bordering a body of water.

32